Names and Nicknames

NAMES AND NICKNAMES
a play by James Reaney

Vancouver, Talonbooks, 1978

published with assistance from the Canada Council

Talonbooks
201 1019 East Cordova
Vancouver
British Columbia V6A 1M8
Canada

This book was typeset by Linda Gilbert of B.C. Monthly Typesetting Service, designed by David Robinson and printed by Hemlock Printers for Talonbooks.

First printing: December 1978

Talonplays are edited by Peter Hay.

Canadian Cataloguing in Publication Data

    Reaney, James, 1926-
      Names and nicknames

    ISBN 0-88922-154-5

    I. Title.
    PS8535.E295N3   jC812'.5'4   C79-091077-2
    PR9199.3.R425N3

Introduction

Names and Nicknames was written with a bare stage in mind. The setting can be accomplished with words, pantomime, the human body, music from rhythm band instruments and the audience themselves. Nothing should stand in the way of a flowing story line that proceeds without a break until the very last chorus. Dress the stage with a stepladder. When Thorntree climbs up on the roof to listen down the chimney, this stepladder is all that is needed. A great many items in the play are meant to be expanded and improvised upon, all the time keeping in mind the insistent rhythm and flow of the story line. For example, try dividing up a chorus with one-half chanting a basic repetitive line while the other half does a whole stanza.

Many of the choruses, by the way, are taken from the suites of words used in a speller that my father learned to spell out of in the 1890's at the Irish School near Stratford, Ontario. The scenery choruses came from such word lists as "In the Yard" and "On the Farm" and the great monumental lists of boys' and girls' names in this book gave me the idea for the climax of the play. Perhaps this might suggest to children plays they could make up from gum cards, telephone directories, even arithmetic books!

All the scenes take place on Farmer Dell's Farm. The time changes from summer to winter, to summer again; then to fall, to winter, and back to summer.

For the opening, the actors could line up before the audience and tell who they are in real life and who they are in the play. Have a discussion with the actors and gradually with the audience about their names — their first, middle and last names. "How many Marys in the audience?" "How many Peters?" Ask what their nicknames are. "Can you guess what my nickname is?" "What it was?" Since the whole business of nicknames is touchy, don't carry this too far. In the Winnipeg production, a very shrewd member of one audience did guess the nickname that one of the actors had lived with as a ten-year-old — "Nelly."

James Reaney
London, Ontario
December, 1973

Names and Nicknames was first performed at the Manitoba Theatre Centre in Winnipeg, Manitoba, in October, 1963, with the following cast:

Mrs. Dell	Martha Henry
Farmer Dell	Heath Lamberts
Etta	Suzanne Grossman
Rob	Nelson Philips
Reverend Hackaberry	Garrick Hagon
Grandpa Thorntree	Ted Hodgeman
Baby One	Anita Cera
Baby Two	Blair Graham
Children	Christine Kirby, Debby Feldbrill
	Craig Parks, Anita Cera
	Blair Graham, Robert Elias
	Sheera Waisman, Angela McLeod
	Meredith Moore, Randy Benson
	Debby Crookes, Sharon Beckstead
	Debby Konowalchuck, Pam Macdonald
	Sherry Israels, Mary Cox
	Nancy Goyman, Joanne Knonpada
	Joanne Gregory, Elizabeth Graham
	Richard Gillman
Soprano Solo	Carla Israels

Directed by John Hirsch and Robert Sherrin
Music by Kenneth Winters
Set and Costume Design by Ted Korol

LIST OF CHARACTERS

OLD GRANDPA THORNTREE, *a trapper.*
FARMER DELL.
FARMER DELL'S WIFE.
COUSIN ETTA, *the hired girl.*
ROB, *the hired man.*
REVEREND HACKABERRY.
BABY ONE.
BABY TWO.
BABY THREE, *a large doll in a christening dress.*
CHORUS, *at least six children.*

PLACE

The hamlet of Brocksden in Southwestern Ontario.

TIME

1900.

CHORUS AND CHIEF ACTORS:
The farm in the morning. The Farm.
Farmer Dell's Farm.

*For the next sequence, the six chief actors mime the words
they are saying. For "copse," they bring uplifted hands
together and someone whistles a bird song. For "barn," they
build a barn, and so on. Not every word gets a gesture and
the whole thing must be kept flowing, but the actors do say
these words with their bodies as well as their mouths.*

CHORUS AND CHIEF ACTORS:
Vale hill dell dale
Bush rock bank field
Pool wood pond creek
Ridge hedge copse yard
Swale lane fence wall
Path road ditch post
Barn shed tree house

Farmer Dell's Farm.

The actors lie down as a rooster crows, some of them on benches. Now, the sleeping DELLS bestir themselves. There can be a mime of dressing, alarm clocks, etc. ROB, the hired man, goes out to get the cows. The CHORUS utter moos and some of them pretend to be cows.

ROB:
> I get up in the morning and go and fetch the cows.
> Cobossy coboss. Cobossy coboss. . . .

Ad lib repetition.

CHORUS: Moo mooo moo moo.

ROB: Come on cushy cows and come to be milked.

CHORUS: Moo.

Select two female members of the CHORUS to be cows.

ROB: *driving the cows with a stick*   Here — here's the
shortest way.

CHORUS: Moo. We have to follow our cowpath.

ROB: And it winds up and down.

CHORUS: Our names are Blossom, Josephine, Moo,
Rachel, Betty, Moo. Next year, let's make the path curve
more here. Rachel, Betty, Blossom and Josephine. Not
too fast or we won't let down our milk.

ROB: Coboss coboss coboss coboss.

CHORUS: Moo.

FARMER DELL: Come cushy cows and we will milk
you.

*FARMER DELL and ROB mime milking the cows with pails
and the CHORUS make milking sounds. The moos and
milking sounds slowly change into the sound of a cream
separator, which ROB turns while FARMER DELL pours in
the milk. An actor turns about pretending to be the revolving
cream separator. Perhaps, over to one side, we see the women
preparing breakfast.*

ROB:
    Turn the separator, turn the separator.
    Cream out one spout. Skim out the other.
    Turn the separator, turn the separator.

CHORUS: The bell goes tink tink tink.

FARMER DELL: If the bell goes, you're turning it too
    slow.

CHORUS: *faster, then fading out*   Tink tink tink
    tink. . . .

ROB: Sorry, Sam. I'm still half asleep.
    Turn the separator, turn the separator.
    Cream out one spout. Skim out the other.
    Turn the separator. . . .

He slows down.

CHORUS: Tink tink.

ROB: *faster*   Cream out one spout. Skim out the other.

*The pig sequence is about to start. This will take some
humility, but it's worth trying. Everyone crouches down at
their troughs and makes a rich oinking sound as FARMER
DELL and ROB feed them.*

FARMER DELL:
  We get up in the morning and fetch the cows
  And then we milk them
  And then I slop the pigs and the cows
  And then I count time
  ONE, FIVE, TEN, FIFTEEN, TWENTY
  Little pigs.

CHORUS:
  One five ten fifteen twenty little pigs.
  Oink oink oink oink oink.

A rising frenzy of sound of pigs at a feeding trough is heard.

FARMER DELL: Hey, Rob! One of them's got away!
  Nineteen little pigs!

They pursue the runaway pig, who leads ROB into the pig wallow — from which he emerges a dripping pillar when the pig is caught and returned.

ROB AND FARMER DELL:
  One, five, ten, fifteen, twenty little pigs.

CHORUS: Oink oink oink oink oink oink.

ROB takes out a harmonica and plays it to the pigs. At certain points in his piece, one pig will stop eating and look up in rapture.

Now, the horse sequence starts. Two of the CHORUS can be the horses. Two of the CHORUS can sit on the bench and drum with noise sticks to imitate the sound of their hooves.

FARMER DELL: Rob, go now and catch the horses.

ROB: Which ones, Sam? Sandy and Charley or Bradley and Dobbin?

FARMER DELL: Today, we're sowing oats and barley,
so hitch up the sorrel horse and Old Charley.

ROB: *with a pail of oats and a rope*   Here Bradley.

He whistles in a neighing way.

ROB: *whistling*   Here Charley.

CHORUS: *two of them galloping about, very hard to
catch*   We won't come. We won't come.
We want to eat grass and play in the sun.

ROB: *whistling*
Here Bradley.
Here Charley.

He whistles at them again.

CHORUS:
We won't come. We won't come.
We want to eat grass and play in the sun.

*With a drum, quite a race can be suggested, but eventually,
after much neighing and hitching, the horses are caught and
hitched to a seed drill — a bench.*

CHORUS, FARMER DELL AND ROB: *interspersed
with each other*
Harnessing horses.
Harnessing horses.
Collar and hames collar and hames
Lift up the neck yoke
Tongue tongue tongue
Tache up the traces to
Whipple trees double trees whipple trees
Whipple trees double trees whipple trees.

ROB: Ouch! You stepped on my foot, Charley.

*FARMER DELL drives off while ROB hops about on one
foot.*

FARMER DELL:
>   Giddup, Bradley. Up there, Charley
>   This oats and barley we've got to be sowing
>   Must get it in so it can start growing
>   Giddup, Bradley. Git up there, Charley
>   Gee! Bradley! Gee! Charley!
>   Haw! Bradley! Haw! Charley!

OLD GRANDPA THORNTREE appears.

*A transition sequence occurs. Don't be afraid to let the
"knee deep" sound carry on.*

*Gradually, it will change into the harsher sound of the
Thorntree sequence.*

CHORUS:
>   So spring on Farmer Dell's Farm.
>   The snow has melted, the snow has gone
>   Tra la la tra la la tra la la
>   The bare trees have put their green leaves on.
>   Tra la la tra la la tra la la
>   Knee deep knee deep knee deep knee deep
>   The frogs in the pond sing
>   Knee deep knee deep knee deep knee deep
>   The frogs in the pond sing.

*The CHORUS hums, a sound interrupted by various farm
noises — a cow mooing, FARMER DELL shouting at the
horses, a bird whistling, a frog song dying away. Slowly, a
chorus of crows cawing is built up and reaches a peak as OLD
GRANDPA THORNTREE enters and dominates the stage.
FARMER DELL and ROB have faded away.*

CHORUS:
>Caw caw caw caw
>Caw caw caw caw
>Raw raw raw raw
>Raw raw raw raw
>Old Grandpa Thorntree. Old Grandpa Thorntree.
>Old Grandpa Thorntree. Old Grandpa Thorntree.

OLD GRANDPA THORNTREE is a ragged, gnarled old man with the remains of a top hat on his head. It is the top hat and the cane that makes him into a thorntree.

When last we saw him, he was one of the horses — one of the men around the Dell farm.

OLD GRANDPA THORNTREE:
>You children always tease me.
>You children always tease me — you kids!

Members of the CHORUS jump forward and mock him.

CHORUS:
>Haw haw haw Old Mr. Thorntree
>Swallowed a peck of rusty nails
>Spits them out and never fails
>To make them twice as rusty
>To make them twice as rusty.
>Swallowed a peck of rusty nails
>Spits them out and never fails
>To make them twice as rusty
>To make them twice as rusty.

OLD GRANDPA THORNTREE: Brat! How can I carry on my profession with you kids putting me in such a bad temper all the time?

CHORUS: What is your profession?

OLD GRANDPA THORNTREE: Being a fence viewer.
I go around seeing that people's fences are straight.

*He uses his stick to line up the CHORUS, who now pretend
to be fenceposts in a fence.*

OLD GRANDPA THORNTREE: Aye — there's where it
goes crooked. It's gone crooked here, too. That post
should be a little to the — a whole sliverful of property
should really be on this side of the fence. Was that post
that way before? I keep thinking of the nasty little tricks
the children played on me at the crossroads coming home
from school — and I can't think straight. All the posts
are out of order. They're all dancing in a circle around
me!

*He turns on the CHORUS who make up a fence, then
dissolve, then make up a fence again.*

OLD GRANDPA THORNTREE: Brat!

CHORUS BOY: What?

OLD GRANDPA THORNTREE: Little girl!

CHORUS BOY: I'm a boy!

OLD GRANDPA THORNTREE: No, you're not. You're a
girl. You certainly resemble a girl. That's a girl's sweater
you're wearing, anyhow. The colours are just a shade too
bright for a boy's sweater.

CHORUS BOY: *dissolving and tearing off his sweater*
Oh — I told Mother I wouldn't wear this sweater. Oh!

CHORUS: Albert's a girl. Albert's a girl. Albert's a girl.

OLD GRANDPA THORNTREE: Now *you're* a boy!

CHORUS GIRL: I am not. I'm a girl!

OLD GRANDPA THORNTREE: *pausing*   Kind of plain for a girl, aren't you?

CHORUS GIRL: Oh boo hoo. Boo hoo.

CHORUS: *turning on her*   Mary's a boy. Mary's a boy!

OLD GRANDPA THORNTREE: Now if any of you ever get feeling cross with one of your playmates and want some assistance in making them feel punk — come to me.

CHORUS:
Caw caw caw caw
Caw caw caw caw
A crow stole Grandpa Thorntree's hat.
Raw raw raw raw
Raw raw raw raw.

They snatch and play ball with OLD GRANDPA THORN-TREE'S battered hat.

CHORUS:
Now he's sorry he called me a brat
And me a girl. And me a boy.

OLD GRANDPA THORNTREE:
Oh I'll never be sorry about that.
Because I'm going to get back at all kids.

CHORUS: *recovering*
Caw caw caw caw.
You'll never get back at us.
You never do and you never did
Caw caw caw caw.

OLD GRANDPA THORNTREE:
    Do me no do's and did me no did's
    I'll get my revenge on some of you kids.

CHORUS:
    Haw haw haw Old Mr. Thorntree
    Swallowed a peck of rusty nails
    And garter snakes with wriggly tails,
    Spits them out and never fails
    To make them twice as rusty
    Twice as wriggly he makes
    The snakes
    And twice as rusty — the nails.

REVEREND HACKABERRY enters.

REV. HACKABERRY: Children, you should not tease
    Mr. Thorntree.

When last seen, REVEREND HACKABERRY, too, was one of the horses.

CHORUS:
    But he's so mean to us, Reverend Hackaberry.
    When he is so mean we cannot be merry.

REV. HACKABERRY:
    But weren't you mean to him first?
    And he cannot help his meanness, you know.

OLD GRANDPA THORNTREE: Oh, I can't, eh? —

He comes out from behind a tree — the stepladder.

OLD GRANDPA THORNTREE:
> I'll get you, Reverend
> I'll some evil to you send,
> For sticking up for me, for trying to help me.
> I don't need your help. I don't need your charity.
> I can view fences in the summer
> And trap animals in the winter.
> And you — you're not youngsters,
> You're all — moungsters and monsters!

He chases the CHORUS away.

REV. HACKABERRY:
> Thorntree, you'll go too far some day,
> And turn into a thorntree by the way.

OLD GRANDPA THORNTREE: How do you know?

REV. HACKABERRY: Look, there's a thorn sticking out of your arm already. I'll swear it grew there.

OLD GRANDPA THORNTREE: *laughing it off*   It did grow there, Hackaberry. It did grow there. And I'll tell the shrikes to put their victim birds on it when it's good and sharp.

OLD GRANDPA THORNTREE exits.

REV. HACKABERRY: *running after him*   Don't run away like that. Thorntree. Come back and listen to reason.

The scene changes to FARMER DELL'S WIFE's kitchen.

Last seen scattering in front of OLD GRANDPA THORN-
TREE'S malice, the CHORUS now re-enter, bearing dishes
and kettles, and other kitchen utensils. One of them bears
a large flashlight tied up in orange cellophane to represent
the setting sun. The CHORUS, with their bodies, build up a
suggestion of the kitchen — they mime windows, cupboards,
doors, and so on. The CHORUS' sunset song should go
quite quickly — despite the slowness of real sunsets.

CHORUS:
>Sunset in Farmwife Dell's kitchen.
>Cups and saucers. Spoons and forks.
>Knives and plates. Tea in kettles.
>Fire in the stove. Bread in the oven.
>Plants in the windows. Wood in the woodbox.
>Towel on the roller. Water in the pail.
>Dipper in the water. Kitchen kitchen
>Supper supper. Sunset sunset.
>Sunset in Mrs. Dell's kitchen
>Sunset in Mrs. Dell's kitchen.

FARMER DELL'S WIFE and COUSIN ETTA enter with
saucepans and dishes. They mime various kitchen tasks,
using members of the CHORUS and their particular utensils.

FARMER DELL'S WIFE: Look, Etta. What a beautiful
sunset! Sam and Rob should soon be in for supper.

COUSIN ETTA: Doesn't the sun gleam pretty on the pots
and pans?

FARMER DELL'S WIFE: Etta, could you take this knife
and go down into the orchard and cut some asparagus?
It'll just be ready.

COUSIN ETTA: Why, a feed of asparagus would be
wonderful for supper.

FARMER DELL: *entering with ROB*   What you got for supper, Mrs. Dell?

FARMER DELL'S WIFE: All sorts of things, Samuel, including some asparagus fresh out of the orchard. Etta is just bringing it up.

FARMER DELL and ROB mime washing and drying themselves.

Everyone at the Dell farm is now bedded down for a good night's sleep — a baby's crying particularly rocks the hired men. At length, morning comes. The CHORUS pretend to be chickens in the henhouse. A cock crows and they all awaken.

DAWN

CHORUS:
Occiocceroccioccer. Occioccericciocceroo.
Time to get up. Time to get up.
Hear about the baby? Heard about the baby?

COUSIN ETTA enters and sprinkles feed for the chickens. Whenever she scatters it, they run and pick it up making hen cackles and any other chicken noises that come to hand.

COUSIN ETTA:
Chook chook chook chook chuokk!
Chook chook chook chook chuokk!
Oh, Sam and Annie. What are you going to name her?

FARMER DELL'S WIFE: We thought Amelia.

COUSIN ETTA: And you're going off to get the Reverend Hackaberry to christen her Amelia? A beautiful name. A beautiful, beautiful name. But, oh, my dear, be careful. I saw old Grandpa Thorntree coming down the road and he looked so mean. He might say something mean about the baby or —

FARMER DELL: I'm not afraid of anything old Grandpa Thorntree can do.

OLD GRANDPA THORNTREE: *suddenly entering* Out of my way, you dratted hens.

The CHORUS all run off.

OLD GRANDPA THORNTREE: Trying to trip me up as usual, you stupid clucks. So you aren't afraid of me, eh, Farmer Dell? Why aren't you afraid of me?

FARMER DELL: I don't know, I'm just not, that's all.

COUSIN ETTA: You clear out of here, Grandpa Thorntree. The very look on your face would sour fresh milk in a pitcher. And you've just kicked two of my best Black Minorcas.

OLD GRANDPA THORNTREE: Oh, a good fat hen likes a playful kick now and then. Well, Farmer Dell and Anne Dell, what are you naming the new little baby?

COUSIN ETTA: Don't tell him. I heard that yesterday he vowed revenge on all the children of the neighbourhood, even the ones that couldn't possibly harm or tease him.

OLD GRANDPA THORNTREE: Why that's not true, Etta dear. I've got a little present for the baby, as a matter of fact. What's its name?

FARMER DELL'S WIFE: She isn't named yet. We're just taking her to be christened.

FARMER DELL: Her name's going to be Amelia.

OLD GRANDPA THORNTREE: Oh. It's going to be Amelia, is it? Well, it isn't I have sworn revenge on every child in the neighbourhood and my special revenge against babies is that I spoil their christenings by thinking up a terrible nickname for them that will stick and stick and stick, it's so sticky. No, they won't call this baby Amelia, though you may christen her that. They'll call her — what does the name Amelia — Mealy! All the children will call her that at school — Oat Mealy!

He goes off laughing and repeating the nickname. The DELLS are thunderstruck.

COUSIN ETTA: Oh, pay no attention to him. Go ahead and have her christened anyhow. Christen her some other name.

FARMER DELL'S WIFE: No, Etta. Her name has to be Amelia. But we can't christen her that until Mr. Thorntree's not around any more. And when will that be? I couldn't bear to send her off to school and have him meet her and say Mealy to her. And the other children might repeat it, too. Oh!

FARMER DELL: What are we going to do, Annie?

FARMER DELL'S WIFE: What can we do but take her back home. No christening today, poor dear.

FARMER DELL: What else can we call her but Baby One. We'll call her that until we can christen her properly.

They exit.

THORNTREE AT THE SCHOOLYARD

The CHORUS comes marching on. As in the first scene, they imitate words with bodily action. They jump across the ditch, for example.

CHORUS:
>A schoolyard a schoolyard a schoolyard
>Where is the schoolyard
>Where the ground is stamped hard
>With the children's stamping feet?
>We're on the way to find it,
>Find it find it
>On the way to school
>Dew dust mud hail
>Snow ice frost smoke
>Road lane ditch track
>Truant officer
>Tree
>Pebble
>Water
>Splash!

The CHORUS divide up into a line of boys and a line of girls and file into school where the teacher and immediate class will be the other five chief actors seated on benches.

IN THE SCHOOL ROOM

FARMER DELL'S WIFE is the schoolmarm. The CHORUS repeats words after her and mimes — or the kids could name the invisible things she points to.

FARMER DELL'S WIFE:
>Desks bell map chart
>Clock book slate globe
>Chalk paper ferrule ouch!
>Blackboard children teacher printer.
>Student satchel pencil crayon
>Register ink-bottle dictionary.

ROB: I'd like to go to school again. I never did my
    Entrance. Etta, the hired girl, is so cruel to me. She says
    I'm such an ignoramus she'd never dream of marrying
    me. But if I could just get my Entrance she might
    consider it. I wonder if the children would let me come
    back.

FARMER DELL'S WIFE AND CHORUS: *using as much*
    mime as possible   What pupils do —
    Read write parse solve
    Think reckon think learn
    Think listen think attend
    Study recite declaim —
    Recollect and reckon compose compute
    Recollect recollect recollect —
    Remembrance remember remembrance
    Calculate analyze.

    There's the Dell's hired man looking in the window!

CHORUS: There's that old Thorntree leaning in the
    other window.

OLD GRANDPA THORNTREE: Listen, kids. He's too
    old to go back to school. And he's too dumb. Just look
    at him. All he knows is how to play the harmonica.

CHORUS: Go away, Rob. You're too old.

ROB: Then how am I to get enough education so Etta
    will marry me? She says I can get my Entrance if I really
    care to. And care for her.

CHORUS: That's just too bad. That's your look out.

OLD GRANDPA THORNTREE: Etta's got her Entrance,
    Rob. Why don't you try some other girl that's not so
    highly educated. There's Leota Throughopper down the
    road. She never got out of Primer Class. She'd have you.
    She's about your speed.

ROB: Well — I guess that's it. I've just set my sights too
       high. And my eyes are turned on too low.

He exits.

*The CHORUS takes over the stage now. We are in the
schoolyard. OLD GRANDPA THORNTREE is watching.*

CHORUS:
      Recess recess! Games games!
      A schoolyard a schoolyard a schoolyard
      Where the ground is hard
      With the stamping children's feet.

They stamp their feet, then break into a games sequence.

CHORUS:
      Crack the Whip!
      Send them flying!
      Prisoner's Base.

Have kids on stilts, playing tug of war, etc.

CHORUS:
      Come pull away, pull away.

      Bull in the ring.

      My bar's made of gold
      My bar's made of iron
      My bar's made of steel
      My bar's made of stone.

Have actual skipping, but watch the knots in those ropes!

CHORUS:
Skipping skipping. The girls are skipping —
Rosy apple lemon pear
These are the colours she should wear.

The boys are walking on stilts.

I am a girl guide dressed in blue
Skipping skipping. The girls are skipping.

For the individual games and skipping rhythms, break the CHORUS up into groups.

CHORUS:
These are the actions I did do
Salute the king. Turn to the queen.

The boys are walking on stilts.

Turn your back on the baseball green
Get down you dirty rascal.

Bluebells cockleshells
Evie ivie over.

My mother said that I was born in January,
February, March, April, May, June, July, August,
September.

A house to let apply within
A woman put out for drinking gin
I call in — *name of the child.*
All in together girls
Very fine weather girls
One two three four five
Salt vinegar mustard pepper
Cedar cider red hot pepper

Hide and go seek. Hide and go seek.

CHORUS:
> Eenie meenie minie moe
> Catch a fat one by his toe
> If he hollers let him go
> Eenie meenie minie moe
> O-U-T spells out and
> OUT you must go.

The child who is "It" counts up to ten and then yells . . .

CHORUS: *("Goal" is pronounced "Gool" in Southern Ontario)*
> Anybody hiding round my gool
> Whether he be hidden or not,
> He shall be caught.
> One two three on Walter!

A sulky CHILD goes over to OLD GRANDPA THORNTREE.

CHILD: Mr. Thorntree. You said if ever we wanted to get back at somebody we might just come to you. Well, those kids haven't let me up to bat yet — what names can I call them?

OLD GRANDPA THORNTREE: Well, you can call 'em . . . . *He whispers.*   And you can —

He whispers.

CHILD: *going over to the CHORUS and starting a name calling sequence*
> Hi — scummy!
> Hi — sissy!

CHORUS:
> Monkey Ape Foxy Toothy
> Fatty Warty Greasy Smelly
> Stinkpot.

Repeat ad nauseum.

The games fade away, and the CHORUS stand moping about listlessly.

CHORUS:
> I won't hold the skipping rope for her
> Not after the nicknames she's called me.
> Hey! Let's make a snowman and then smash him to bits!
> Winter isn't finished yet
> The frogs have stopped singing!

They have invisible snowballs. But as the snowballs fly, we still hear the first song.

CHORUS:
> A schoolyard a schoolyard a schoolyard
> Where is the schoolyard
> Where the ground is stamped hard
> With the children's stamping feet?
> We're on the way to find it.

The sound of stamping feet is heard.

CHORUS:
> Find it find it
> On the way to school
> Dew dust mud hail
> Snow ice frost smoke
> Road lane ditch track
> Truant officer
> Tree
> Pebble
> Water
> Splash!

ANOTHER BABY AT THE DELLS

If one of the girls is really good at skipping, you might have a skipping cadenza here using one of the skipping rhymes to finish the schoolyard scene with. Perhaps a fade-out to suggest that the skipping girl goes on forever. Perhaps the "January, February" skipping song should melt here into the time bridge.

CHORUS:
  Two years later in the summer
  Two years later in the summer
  Summer summer summer summer
  Another little baby was born
  While the birds were singing.

Bird whistles of various sorts are heard here.

CHORUS:
  And Queen Anne's Lace was blossoming
  And ox-eyed daisy fading
  And raspberries ripening
  And honey bees humming.

The humming of bees continues here for some time.

CHORUS:
  Beneath the golden sun
  Beneath the golden sun
  Two years later in the summer
  Summer summer summer summer
  Another babe was born — while

Bird whistles and then bee hums are heard here.

CHORUS: While while while while —

ROB and FARMER DELL enter, miming the making of haycocks.

ROB: I never thought I'd see us making this hay, it's been raining so. But the rain sloped off at last.

FARMER DELL: Another forkful of that coil, Rob.

ROB: What are you naming the new boy, Sam?

FARMER DELL: Well — we thought and we thought. It has to be a name that Grandpa Thorntree can't make a horrible nickname of.

ROB: Yessirree. There's twenty babies without names in this neighbourhood and all because of him and his terrible tongue.

FARMER DELL: We couldn't name him Abel.

ROB: No. You couldn't name him Abel.

FARMER DELL: Because then Thorntree would sneer — Unable.

ROB: Why so he would. So he would.

FARMER DELL: We couldn't call him John. Because old Grandpa Thorntree might call him Jack in the Pulpit or even worse — Jackass.

ROB: It would be just like him to do that.

FARMER DELL: So what we're going to do is have Reverend Hackaberry come over to the house at dinner time so we won't have to take the baby out onto the road to the church where we might meet old Thorntree, and we're giving the baby five names, five names, so if even he hears the names, he can't possibly spoil five names all at once and we'll call the baby by the name he doesn't have time to get out.

REVEREND HACKABERRY enters.

REV. HACKABERRY: Well, Sam, what have you decided to call this baby boy of yours?

FARMER DELL: We're going to call him Paul John Peter James Martin.

REV. HACKABERRY: Yes. That's very wise in view of the difficulty with Thorntree. Let us repair to your house then; and Rob, you might pump a pail of fresh cold water to christen this child with. Good day, Annie. Good day, Etta, and good day, Baby One.

BABY ONE should be played by a member of the CHORUS.

FARMER DELL'S WIFE and COUSIN ETTA enter with a doll as the new baby. BABY ONE is now a little girl. ROB mimes pumping and OLD GRANDPA THORNTREE begins to climb up the stepladder or, if you like, onto the roof of the house, where he listens down the chimney. A member of the CHORUS can be the pump.

CHORUS:
    Down underground it's cold as winter
    Down at the bottom of the well
    Pump pump pump pump
    Pump pump pump pump
    Up above it's fire hot summer
    The sun like a golden butter nut
    Pump pump pump pump
    Pump pump pump pump
    Pump up winter into summer
    From the secret underground stream
    That flows beneath us like a dream
    Pump! Splash! Gurgle gurgle.
    Pump pump pump pump
    Gurgle gurgle gurgle gurgle.

The family arrange themselves and ROB brings in the pail of water. OLD GRANDPA THORNTREE is now at the top of the stepladder.

REV. HACKABERRY: And now, Farmer Dell, what names do you give this child. This little man?

OLD GRANDPA THORNTREE: Names? I wish they'd clear their chimney better so I could hear properly. Names?

FARMER DELL'S WIFE: Did you hear something on the roof?   *To the audience, inviting their participation.* Does anyone hear anything on the roof?

The children in the audience may tell her about OLD GRANDPA THORNTREE, but just as she looks, he ducks down his head.

FARMER DELL'S WIFE: No, I guess there isn't anybody up there.

With careful control, the audience can again be brought in here. Every time they point out OLD GRANDPA THORN-TREE, by the time she turns round, he has ducked down. Ad lib to the temperature of the occasion.

FARMER DELL: It's the fir tree scraping against the shingles in the summer breeze. I name this child Paul.

CHORUS: Paul.

FARMER DELL: John Peter James Martin.

The CHORUS repeat the other names after FARMER DELL.

REV. HACKABERRY: *taking the baby*   And now little baby I name thee —

OLD GRANDPA THORNTREE: Five names! Too many names. Fat name. Too many names. Fat name. Yah! Fat Name, Fat Name!

He opens his umbrella and leaps off the roof.

FARMER DELL'S WIFE: Oh, Sam! He was up on the roof listening to us down through the chimney. He heard the baby's names!

OLD GRANDPA THORNTREE: That makes the twenty-first child whose name I've ruined.   *He laughs.*

FARMER DELL: Sic the dogs on him. Sic him, Rover. Sic him, Bluebell. Sic him, Daisy. Sic him, Rollo. Get him, Gnasher.

Members of the CHORUS leap forward.

CHORUS:
Bow wow wow! Bow wow wow!
Grr grrr grr! Grr grr grr!
Bow wow wow! Bow wow wow!
Bite him, fellow. Bite him!

They chase OLD GRANDPA THORNTREE around the stage and finally off. If he goes through the audience, you're going to get audience participation, which should be carefully handled.

FARMER DELL: You'd better whistle the dogs back, Rob, before he does something to them.

ROB: *whistling*   Here, Rover. Come on back. Here, Bluebell. Back you silly dogs. You're no match for Thorntree. It's no use. They won't come back for my whistle, and he's hitting them with his cane.

FARMER DELL: We need more whistlers. Anybody here good at whistling dogs back for us?   *The audience whistles.*   Louder and higher than that.

There are renewed efforts to get the dogs back. The dogs reluctantly return. Perhaps they run off again, in which case the audience has to whistle them back again.

FARMER DELL: Thatta boy, Rover. Thatta boy, Rollo.

FARMER DELL'S WIFE: What will we call this baby, Sam?

FARMER DELL: I guess we'll have to call him Baby Two.

FARMER DELL'S WIFE: Baby Two. I couldn't bear to have a child called — Fat Name.

COUSIN ETTA: I think we should get the village constable.

FARMER DELL'S WIFE: Reverend Hackaberry, what are we going to do if we have another baby and cannot name it either? Nor apply for a birth certificate for them?

REV. HACKABERRY: Let us all go to the church and pray about it. Come with me. God will surely suggest something. We'd better speak in sign language just in case there might be listeners — behind that thicket — in the ditch, underneath us in the culvert. So — speak in sign language. Now at first, Sam and Annie, you tried this — *He holds his hands a small space apart as if telling a fish story.*   Then this last time —   *He holds his hands a wider distance apart.*   But the next time, the methods we use against Grandpa Thorntree must be this —

He stretches his hands way apart, then whispers in their ears.

FARMER DELL AND FARMER DELL'S WIFE: First we
tried this —   *They gesture.*   Then we tried this —
A larger gesture.   Next time try this —

The biggest gesture.

*Have the gesturing and whispering repeated among the whole
cast.*

FARMER DELL: It will take some study. Why, there
must be hundreds of them.

FARMER DELL'S WIFE: It will not only take some
study, but also the production of a third child. Where
shall we find that?

REV. HACKABERRY: Both can be found. Meanwhile,
as I see it, the problem is not to be solved this way —
Repeating the first gesture.   But only in this way —
The final gesture.   But let us go up to the church and
pray.

*REVEREND HACKABERRY and FARMER DELL and his
WIFE exit.*

IN THE FALL

*Across the stage, the CHORUS blow like falling leaves. The
main characters return to mime the fall.*

ALL: Fall and harvest on the farm.

Rye oats	Mangel wurzels
Wheat barley	Turnips corn
Apple pears	Geese and hogs
Chaff straw	Sheaf stook
Pumpkins buckwheat	Potatoes grain
Ducks drakes	Chicks parsnips.

Scything, turnip pulling, and stooking can be mimed here.

ALL:

Crops and roots   Crops and roots
Granary full   Root cellar full
Silo full   Cellar full
Harvest harvest   Harvest harvest
Fall fall fall fall
Autumn autumn autumn autumn.

They hum and whistle like the wind. The CHORUS whirl by again. Part of the group chant, "The leaves are leaving the groves," underneath the following lines. Later on, select another repeat line and chant it under.

ALL:

Oak leaves falling fir needles stay
Ash leaves falling birch birch
The elms are golden and soon are bare
Beech leaves are brown and beechnuts are ripe
The leaves are leaving the groves
Under the grey sky, the bare woods and
The squirrel's asleep and the ground
Smoke from the chimney and frost on the ground.
The stream is still with
Still still
Ice Ice Ice Ice.

The idea of things that are flowing suddenly still. They make the wind sound again and sprinkle snow from their hands. OLD GRANDPA THORNTREE enters wearing snowshoes. This is his moment of triumph, and the members of the CHORUS can be the various animals in his traps. Being caught in the traps can be mimed.

OLD GRANDPA THORNTREE:
> While the other people sink in the snowy ooze
> I float above it on my snowshoes
> And everybody's afraid of me
> And everybody respects me
> While other people sink in the snowy ooze
> I float above it on my snowshoes
> Fifty unchristened babies, ha ha!
> Nameless but nicknameful
> Even the children with their names
> Dread my tongue's destroying flames
> And now I'll see what my traps are doing.

He bats each animal into a heap in the centre of the stage as he speaks.

OLD GRANDPA THORNTREE:
> Ah! Here's a rabbit the steel is chewing
> Rabbit foot not so lucky, eh?
> Well, stay there!
> Well, what have we here ready for a box
> But a full grown red-coated black-tailed fox
> Get over there!
> What have you caught old rusty spring?
> Why, I do believe, two priceless ermine!
> Get over there!
> And what's in you my favourite trap?
> Why, guess — a ferocious old bobcat.
> Get over there!
> Hurray!
> I'll have to go off to get my sleigh
> To haul my trapped animals away
> And then I'll skin them, ha ha ha,
> And then I'll sell them — ha ha ha!
> While other people sink in the snowy ooze,
> I float above it on my snowshoes.

*He exits, or optionally, the animals put him into a frenzy
by escaping from his traps. The stage darkens and the
CHORUS rises from the heap with lighted flashlights, which
they move about like winter stars.*

CHORUS:
> Stars on a frosty night
> In the depth of winter
> Stars on a frosty night
> In the depth of winter.

*If each child has two flashlights, quite a few constellations
can drift over the stage: the Big Dipper, Cassiopeia's Chair,
and, last of all — Orion.*

CHORUS:
> Shine on the sleeping fields
> Sleep beneath the snow
> On the trees turned upsidedown
> Their sap sunk below
> Orion, Orion, Orion, Orion,
> The cruel sworded giant
> Made of stars he marches on
> Over the snowy world.
>
> Stars on a frosty night
> In the depth of winter
> Stars on a frosty night
> In the depth of winter.

*A rooster crows, and it becomes light again. Bird whistles are
heard.*

CHORUS:
> Spring on Farmer Dell's farm
> The snow has melted, the snow has gone
> Tra la la tra la la tra la la
> The bare trees have put their green leaves on.
> Tra la la tra la la tra la la
> Knee deep knee deep knee deep knee deep
> The frogs in the pond sing
> Knee deep knee deep knee deep knee deep
> The frogs in the pond sing.

*The CHORUS hum and occasionally say "knee deep"
under the following dialogue. They fade into less distinct
"knee-deeps" and change into trees and fence posts along
the road.*

THE THIRD BABY

ROB: *as if walking into town*   Oh, dear me. I've got the
time off to go in and write the examination. I shall never
be able to enter the building. As to entering the room,
they'll all be young kids twelve or fourteen, and here I
am eighteen. I'll tower over them like a bean pole. They'll
be people younger'n me writing their University
Entrance, let alone the High School Entrance. I've
got to quiet my mind with something — I'll see
if I can kick this stone all the way into town —
I never knew I had nerves till now — if I can kick it all
the way into town, that means I'll pass the exam, but
if I — let's see. I'll go over the Arithmetic rules in my
head and then I'll do my memory work. A number
that divides two or more numbers exactly is called —

He kicks the stone about in a circle.

OLD GRANDPA THORNTREE: *picking up the stone*
Talking to himself. The first sign of advanced madness.

ROB: You give me that stone!

OLD GRANDPA THORNTREE: Ah, a special stone, eh?
    You intend kicking it all the way into town and if you
    don't lose it, you'll pass, eh? Well, you're going to lose it.
    Unless —

ROB: Unless what?

OLD GRANDPA THORNTREE: Unless you tell me
    what's been going on at the Dell farmhouse lately.

ROB: I won't tell you anything.

OLD GRANDPA THORNTREE: I'll follow you all the
    way into town telling people how old you are and what
    exam you're trying.

ROB: I don't care.

OLD GRANDPA THORNTREE: I'll look in the window
    at you — I'll keep saying to myself, but you'll hear it —
    "Wrong, Rob, wrong, Rob."

ROB: Oh —

OLD GRANDPA THORNTREE: I only want to know
    one thing, Rob. Is there a new baby at the Dell's?

ROB: No. Not that I've heard of.

OLD GRANDPA THORNTREE: *laughing*   And is it
    going to be christened today?

ROB: No. It is not!

OLD GRANDPA THORNTREE: *throwing back the
    stone*   That's all I want to know. That's all I want
    to know.

ROB: Oh, you old devil.   *He picks up the stone and
    rushes off.*   Now he'll ruin that baby's name too.

The DELL FAMILY march out of their house. FARMER DELL is holding the third and latest baby. BABY ONE and BABY TWO are walking now.

OLD GRANDPA THORNTREE: Well, Farmer Dell. So this is the latest little Dell. And all the family with you. BABY ONE and BABY TWO, I see. Hello BABY ONE.

BABY ONE: You are a bad man, Grandpa Thorntree.

BABY TWO: Mooly moo dirly irly a doidle.

OLD GRANDPA THORNTREE: Yes, and where might you all be going? Off to church, perhaps?

FARMER DELL: We're going off to church to get our children christened.

OLD GRANDPA THORNTREE: And what are you going to name them? These two's names I know — Oat Mealy, wasn't it? And Fat Name or too many names or Fatty for short. You might as well tell me what you're going to name this infant right now. So I can tell you what nickname I'll brand it with if you dare christen it.

REV. HACKABERRY: *entering with a basin of water* What names do you give these children, Samuel and Ann Dell?

The CHORUS enter with REVEREND HACKABERRY. Later, they block off OLD GRANDPA THORNTREE'S escape.

FARMER DELL: This one's to be Amelia. This one's Paul John Peter James Martin, and I want to name this one —

OLD GRANDPA THORNTREE: Yes, yes. Let's hear the ridiculous name so you can stop the christening party before it's too late.

42

FARMER DELL: We're going to call our third boy
    baby —

A drum underlines the growing river of names.

FARMER DELL:
    Aaron Abel Abijah Abner
    Abraham Adam Adolphus Albert
    Alexander Alfred Algernon Alonzo
    Alvin Ambrose Amos Andrew
    Anthony Archibald Arnold Arthur
    Asa Augustus.

FARMER DELL'S WIFE:
    Baldwin Basil
    Benedict Benjamin Bernard Bertram
    Caleb Calvin Cecil Cephas
    Charles Christopher Clarence Clement
    Cornelius Cuthbert Cyril Cyrus.

BABY ONE: Daniel David Donald.

BABY TWO: Dionysius.

ROB:
    Duncan Ebeneezer Edgar Edmund
    Edward Edwin Egbert Eli
    Elias Elijah Enoch Ephraim
    Erastus Ernest Eugene Eustace
    Ezekiel Ezra Felix Ferdinand
    Francis Franklin Frederic.

COUSIN ETTA:
    George
    Gideon Gilbert Godfrey Gregory.

OLD GRANDPA THORNTREE: Stop stop stop stop.

COUSIN ETTA:
  Gustavus Guy Harold Henry
  Herbert Herman Hezekiah Hiram
  Horace Horatio Hubert Hugh
  Humphrey Hugo Ira Isaac.

FARMER DELL: And also Jabez Jacob James.

CHORUS:
  Jasper Jerome Jesse Job
  Jobin Jonas Jonathan Joseph.

OLD GRANDPA THORNTREE:
  Stop stop stop stop
  I cannot stand all these names
  Names names names names.

He sinks to the ground, then shoots up and begins to dance a thorntree dance to the names.

FARMER DELL'S WIFE: Joshua Josiah Julius Justin.

CHORUS:
  Lambert Lawrence Lemuel Leonard
  Levi Lewis Lionel Lorenzo
  Lucius Luke Luther.

ROB:
  Mark
  Marmaduke Matthew Maurice Martin
  Michael Miles Morgan Moses.

BABY ONE;   Nathan Nathaniel Nicholas.

BABY TWO: Norman.

COUSIN ETTA: Octavius Oliver Orlando Oscar.

CHORUS:
  Patrick Paul Peleg Peter
  Philip Phineas oh — oh.

They hum as everyone gathers up speed.

FARMER DELL:
Ralph Raphael Raymond Reginald Reuben.

CHORUS:
Richard Robert Roderic Roger Roland.

FARMER DELL'S WIFE:
Rufus Rupert Samson Samuel Saul.

CHORUS:
Seth Silas Silvanus Silvester Simeon.

FARMER DELL:
Simon Solomon Stephen Sydney Thaddeus.

CHORUS: Theodore!

FARMER DELL:
Theophilus Thomas Timothy Urban.

CHORUS: Vincent!

FARMER DELL: Walter Zachariah!

By this time OLD GRANDPA THORNTREE has danced himself off the stage.

REV. HACKABERRY: Quick, Rob. Go and see what's happened to the old trapper. I thought I saw him fall down there.

FARMER DELL: It worked. We named old Grandpa Thorntree so many names he couldn't think of a nickname. Couldn't think of anything towards the last there, but just to get away.

ROB: *bringing in a dead thorntree*   Well, look what's happened to him. He's changed into a thorntree, at least I think he has.

COUSIN ETTA: That's his hat, and there's his cane.

FARMER DELL'S WIFE: How did he do that?

REV. HACKABERRY: He was so balked, his envy and
spite were so frustrated that they turned in upon
themselves and produced this awful miracle.

BABY ONE: Poor old Grandpa Thorntree.

FARMER DELL'S WIFE: Don't you dare touch that dead
tree, Amelia. It might still hurt you! Amelia — I can call
her by her rightful name. And Paul. Little Paul, I can call
you by your name now. And which of his hundred names
will we call this little dear?

FARMER DELL: Whichever the first name I said was.

FARMER DELL'S WIFE: Aaron. Little Aaron who struck
the rock and forth came water.

REV. HACKABERRY: Think of all the other babies who
can now be properly christened.

COUSIN ETTA: But now we must go home and have
enough christening dinner for three little christened ones.
But where were you this afternoon, Rob? We missed you.

ROB: I was to town. Etta, do you see this stone?

COUSIN ETTA: I certainly do. Is there anything extra-
special about it?

ROB: When I was walking into town today to write my
examination, I said to myself, "If I can kick this stone
all the way into town and back, I'll probably pass." And
I did. And you know how hard that is.

COUSIN ETTA: Yes, Rob.

ROB: If it turns out I did pass the Entrance examination, will you marry me?

COUSIN ETTA: Rob, I've been thinking, I'll marry you whether you pass it or not. Now that Grandpa Thorntree is gone, it's safe to get married and have babies with proper names again. That's really what was troubling me.

FARMER DELL'S WIFE: So we must make this a betrothal party as well as a christening party. What will we eat at this party?

The words are arranged in a "Turkey in the Straw" pattern, which the six chief actors dance while the CHORUS chants. A dance of girls with dolls is a possibility here, since all the young children in the district can now be properly christened.

CHORUS:
Oh — buns and rolls, soups and teas
Sauces and pies, sauces and pies
Stews and muffins, biscuits waffles
Butter and pastries, porridge and milk.
Pancakes and crackers, doughnuts, dumplings
Pancakes and crackers, doughnuts, dumplings
Blanc mange puddings sandwiches cocoa
And other good things to eat, to eat.

Everyone laughs. Then switch the mood to —

CHORUS:
Vale hill dell dale
Path road ditch post
Barn shed tree house
Long ago long ago on
Farmer Dell's Farm.

TALONBOOKS — THEATRE FOR THE YOUNG 1978

Raft Baby — Dennis Foon
The Windigo — Dennis Foon
Heracles — Dennis Foon
A Chain of Words — Irene Watts
Apple Butter — James Reaney
Geography Match — James Reaney
Names and Nicknames — James Reaney
Ignoramus — James Reaney
A Teacher's Guide to Theatre for Young People —
     Jane Baker, ed.
A Mirror of Our Dreams — Joyce Doolittle and Zina Barnieh